the light that signals home

Kendra Wong

Presentation by *BookLeaf Publishing*

Web: www.bookleafpub.com

E-mail: info@bookleafpub.com

ISBN: 9789358313307

First edition 2023

dedicated to my loving family. papa, momma, your support means the world to me, in writing and life.

nini, I hope I make you half as proud as you always make me. my shining star <3

ACKNOWLEDGEMENT

Firstly, I have to thank my family. Papa, you're my #1 investor and I hope the return is worthy. (I'm sorry for swearing.) Momma, when I released my first book you were my biggest fan and you will never know how much that meant to me. Nini, I could write pages of how much I love you, but it'll never be enough. You're the best part of my life and your love brings me so much joy. Your big sis will always be proud of you. You're the best part of my life and your big sis will always be proud of you.

Big thank you to my friends who kept me afloat and helped me grow as a person while this book was being written. You all had to listen to me moan and cry about a MAN *and* you helped me hold onto my happiness so... you guys are the realest. Special thanks to Zak for helping me with the book cover.

Maxime, you are the light at the end of the tunnel and I can't believe that you're mine. Thank you for supporting me, for reading every piece of poetry I cautiously shared, for loving me through every moment of doubt. Thank you for being my muse and my love.

And thank you to every single person who read this. You're probably just family and friends, but you're here. I love you all so much.

PREFACE

After my first big break up I wrote poems, infinite poems, to help me process my thoughts. I wrote about ignoring my feelings, about diving into them, and about the rage I felt. I was lost for a while after, and I made mistakes. Some of the poems are titled after words I learned that aptly describe the emotion I'm trying to capture in my poem. Audre Lorde wrote that poetry is "illumination, for it is through poetry that we give name to those ideas which are, until the poem, nameless - about to be birthed, but already felt." That is what poetry has done for me, and I hope that it can do the same for you. This book is a collection of some of the poems I wrote, detailing the heartbreak and all the conflicting feelings I felt after, but most importantly the fact that there is a light at the end of the tunnel every single time I was lost. I found my light, and I hope you will find yours.

all my love.

is it a break up or the end of the world?

come and kiss me my dear,
come hold me close
before the world falls apart,
I'd not like to be morose.
I know i know,
it's not so dramatic.
but can you blame me?
I don't want us shelved, stored in the attic.
saying goodbye is so difficult,
when you don't want time to end,
I know this is what must be,
but I don't think my heart will ever mend.
how will we end, do you think?
will it be an ember going out?
or will it be like fireworks, raining from the
heavens?
all I know is it's you I can't live without
hopefully in another life I'll find you again
some alternate timeline
where things didn't come an end
and every morning I'll wake up to you as mine

phantom limb

you made precise incisions
cut away all the tragic parts of me
and after you cut the final piece
you left, fickle as you are
'phantom limb' for veterans
just like I feel the phantoms of you

in every love song I trace the lyrics
like I traced your skin
all the happy endings used to be ours
everyone I meet a liar in my eyes
but everyday I search for what we shared

that love, that love, that love.

I wish I had never fallen from the skies
into your arms and your eyes
I've searched for that light in everyone after

I wish I had never fallen into sweet sin
so that I would never have to feel this loss
as if I walk around with you attached
I can feel you so close I could touch your cheek
but when I look to my side, you're missing

where did my limb go?

saudade

every memory but this one,
the one that makes it hard to forget.
blue sweater, black jeans
your eyes jewels in the dim lights
you said your hair was messy,
but I thought it was young and boyish
paired with a heartbreaker of a smile

just over an hour of conversation,
you felt like a dream
felt like a lifeline
felt like sanctuary.
and the way you looked at me
made me pinch my skin
because I couldn't believe the possibility
of you
loving me.

my sunshine spilled over my skin
when you filled me with a piece of your past
and the heart of a child
while you smiled I was breathless
visions of things i never wanted
I suddenly do.

everything gone upside down
and if this was the end of all things
i would watch the earth collapse for this hour

world spinning out of control
thinking
"I searched my whole life for this
this is the sun on my face
god I hope I get to look at you for the rest of my
days"
because the love held in those eyes
and that melting smile
I would have died on the battlefield for

every memory has a marked grave in my
cemetery of us
but your blue sweater and black jeans refuse to
be buried
because while I wake up searching for peace
under the empty circadian skies,
it sits in an open casket
so I may walk over and mourn
and feel the earth collapse under my feet.

something old

everyone tells me
fall in love with a man who brings you joy
fall in love with a man who is kind to everyone
fall in love with a man who makes an effort
what if I did?
what happened to him?
what happened to the man I fell in love with?
so perfect by everyone's standards
but so quick to give up
so sudden
something amiss
your lips locked with no key in sight
but you don't fool me
preaching your gospel
don't treat me like a child
have a little respect
I have none for you
just fragments of memories with someone else
who wears your features and has your laugh
social standards must be nonsense
because you fit them perfectly
but still left me empty and broken
for what?

regret

I hope when you tell them about me
your words pour out like honey
and everyone sighs
hearing of a love perfectly ripe on the vine
because I couldn't bear knowing
you're full of

who's mourning us?

if he had ever loved me,
I'd know.
I'd feel it in my heart down to my toes
I wouldn't be looking around for signs
in a room filled with people dressed in black
standing around, mourning us
but the box is empty
because we're not sure
there ever was anything to burn

and as the pine gets lowered into dark earth
I think I heard a thump or a plea
but it's muffled
as fresh dirt spreads over worn wood.

midnight café

if she could go back
she would've kissed him
in that parking lot
under the moon's shine
peeking through the clouds
what a sight, she said
but she wasn't looking at the moon
not at all

she never wanted anything serious
only wanted to live in the bliss
something to make the hot summer days
pass by with ease
temporary, she said
something to look forward to every day
someone to look forward to every night

it's not worthy of attention now
only a few weeks of her life
she'll find someone else
something to fill her with butterflies
chase her demons away
live her life under the lights
for what's left of her glimmering summer

kairos

but
my dear
what if all I want to do is kiss you?

forget everything else,
forget all the reasons for us not to
come trace my smile with your lips

it'll be our little secret.

ache

don't look now
he looks like the stars hung in the sky
tension sewn into the fabric of the air
hands shaking like addicts
(maybe we are.)

if I reach out and touch would it kill us
but it kills me just look
and see a momentary glimpse, the fleeting gaze
does he feel the earth's magnetic field as well
pulling me across the room
for a paintbrush whisper of our knuckles
almost enough to bring me to my knees

locked lips, locked door
no we shouldn't
hands under his suit
hands in my hair
can't breathe can't think
we shouldn't
but we do
we always do.

therefore i am

who am I?
without you I am not who I thought
late nights trying to hide in another's eyes
running as fast as I can before it catches up
why is it that you blame me so?
I am adrift and afraid
that I am no one without your love
that my art and music were stolen by you

yet i still stand here
seeing the beauty in the sun's rise and fall

I am a woman
who loved and lost
who is funny and kind
a lover and a fighter
and I'll be just fine on my own
knowing exactly who I am

compare and contrast

you wanna know how it feels
let me give you a taste
come close, ex-lover
and I'll tell you the truth

it feels like the sun on my face
after days of being stuck in the blackness
like loving and being loved is not work
but instead an effortless dance
weeks passing by without worries
like this love is all the colours of the rainbow
and it envelops my grey limbs with it
it feels like the first breath of fresh air
and yet like the smell of home

it's different this time
not because it wasn't love before
but because this type of love
from this version of myself
is like nothing else before
and I can't imagine anything else
being just as exquisite as this.

something new

keep me up all night
I wont mind
yeah, I've got class in the morning
no, let's not go to sleep
let's share our secrets on the hardwood floor
and laugh loud enough to wake the neighbours
throwing popcorn at each other
'oh you're such an asshole'
(but I don't mean it,
most of the time.)
maybe a wine glass or two
cheap wine (but its my favourite brand.)
and when I get sleepy
I'll fall asleep to the sound of your heartbeat
enveloped in your warmth

when did you start to feel like home?

heraclitus

the sound of soft breathing echoes in the room
knowing he's asleep gives me time to breathe
his curls are soft underneath my fingertips,
I pick and pull at them mindlessly,
picking and pulling at my thoughts

fear runs deep, deeper than I know,
taking over like instinct, a fight or flight
response

wondering what I'm doing,
lying here when I wrote an oath to myself

it's not too late to disappear
pull back before he's rooted in my earth
if only to shield what's left of me

but if not now, when?

how far can I run?
how close can I stay?
there's a question mark on my intentions
but it's enough to live on smiles and laughs
while I follow the river's current
in search of my missing answers

you can never step into the same river twice
change will always take place
the water will be different this time around

anagapesis

he was right
I love looking over and seeing your blue hoodie
muscles tightened around the wheel
dark skies still illuminating your pretty face
eyes on the road but mine rest on you

a lifetime ago I thought it'd be him
and my thoughts can't help but wander
back to my promises of old
and the joy of young hope
but the warmth of your hand resting on my thigh
and the soft upturn of your lips
settles something in my chest

because ill kiss nostalgia
but I'll never love it the same way.

I apologize for drifting away
I can't suppress my memories
and all that come with it
but I'll write you a truth
and print it in every paper
that it brings me infinitely more joy
that I'm in this car with you
cause damn
I love that look you get
when you look back and catch my gaze.

02:21

he opened my eyes to so many new colours
when I was stuck in the grey
and I love that he's gentle with my heart
when I fear the burn he soothes my aches

and his friends, oh they love me
not lost in jealousy, but glad to see him so happy
so excited to listen to him talk about me
so welcoming to my presence (and my flaws)

and my mind still can't wrap around the idea
that I have freedom
that I'm free to go out with my friends
and when I asked for permission he laughed,
"love, they're your friends. why are you asking
me?"

I was so used to being trapped in my box
and when I was scared to communicate
he spoke to me with a kindness I've never known
all my fears the leaves in fall

I never realized that I'd traded myself for
someone else
and I was happy to do it in my past but

I think I've realized that
this is how it's supposed to be.

monday nightmare

you sat across from me
silverware clinking on glass
people chatting all around
her hand laced in yours
pretty smile, golden hair
a deep rumble next to me
his hand laced in mine
it's hard to meet your irises
I feel the burn of your gaze
her smile is softer than mine
do you like that more
the air is thick in my lungs
my feet take me far
but your warmth corners me at the door
my eyes snag on your lips
and your beautiful face fractures with pain
I breathe you in
and the scent of *home*
breaks me

you asked me why

you can't quantify why
neither can I
but I'm going to try

because I love the way the sun hits your eyes
and the crinkles around them too
and I think it's beautiful everytime you try
to pull me out of my mind that's oh so blue
and I think I like it when you come by
just to kiss me even though I caught the flu
and it was cool that you gave me my first taste
of pumpkin pie
because I'm planning all my dad's dishes for you
I find it crazy that you always give me
butterflies
I'm terrified because of him that it'll be you too
but instead you just leave me tonguetied
everytime you say you've discovered something
about me that's new
cause it feels better than the next high
and I've never heard a word from you that's
untrue

but most of all it's amazing that despite how I try
you refuse to say goodbye
and why, I haven't got a clue.

from him.

je sens la douceur de ta peau
sur mes lèvres quand je t'embrasse l'odeur de ton
parfum sur mon nez quand on se caresse et je me
dis
si le paradis existe
j'y suis

(I feel the softness of your skin
on my lips when I kiss you
the smell of your perfume on my nose when we
caress
and I say to myself
if heaven exists
I'm there.)

altar

he's got cheekbones
that cut my heart open
and he's unlike any other
with jeans that fit *oh so right*
and eyelashes that brush my skin
everywhere he leaves a kiss

I could drown in his arms
I could love him to death
but I've never so come alive
he's just a man
but in the light I can see his halo
and beneath his reverent words
I can see his wings
let's go somewhere they aren't
where we can hide from our sins

maybe I'll give my life for this
I know I'll give my love to you

I pray for this forever

lifetimes with you

we're so young
what we are is even younger
and yet I've lived lifetimes in your arms
slept years in your bed

I want to spend the eons being yours
every trace of your skin is a welcome home
like we were written to meet
in the crowded mall
by fate itself

centuries from now we'll become nothing
just constellations in the sky
astronomers will study our hearts
sew stories from our lives
they'll never know us
not without the tragedy of death

because in our moments of life
we created a home that
will be lost to everyone but us

they might say we're beautiful
as twinkling stars
but we'll never be more stunning than we are
right now in our youth

the light at the end of the tunnel

the world will tell you
there's nothing left
but they're wrong
everything will be just right